HEXAGRAMS

A Poet's Journey
Through the I Ching

HEXAGRAMS
A Poet's Journey
Through the I Ching

Donald Beagle

[signature]

with 64 chromotints by

Meredith Joy Merritt

[signature]

library
partners
press

ISBN 978-1-61846-138-4

Hexagrams: A Poet's Journey Through the I Ching

Copyright © 2023 Donald Beagle

Illustrated chromotints by Meredith Joy Merritt

Produced and distributed by
Library Partners Press
Wake Forest University
1834 Wake Forest Road
Winston-Salem, North Carolina 27106

library
partners
press

www.librarypartnerspress.org

Manufactured in the United States of America

This book is dedicated to the memory of Marshall Ho'o, Professor of Oriental History
California Institute of the Arts

"...writing consists no longer in narrating but in saying that one is narrating, and what one says becomes identified with the very act of saying....The world in its various aspects is increasingly looked upon as discrete rather than continuous....Thought, which until the other day appeared to us as something fluid, evoking linear images such as a flowing river or an unwinding thread...we now tend to think of as a series of discontinuous states....By what route is the soul or history or society or the subconscious transformed into a series of black lines on a white page?...The person 'I,' whether explicit or implicit, splits into a number of different figures: into an 'I' who is writing and an 'I' who is written, into an empirical 'I' who looks over the shoulder of the 'I' who is writing and into a mythical 'I' who serves as a model for the 'I' who is written. The 'I' of the author is dissolved in the writing."

—ITALO CALVINO
CYBERNETICS AND GHOSTS

"...I have projected my subjective contents into the symbolism of the hexagrams...the Chinese picture of the moment encompasses everything down to the minutest nonsensical detail, because all of the ingredients make up the observed moment...synchronicity takes the coincidence of events in space and time as meaning something more than mere chance, namely, a peculiar interdependence of objective events among themselves as well as with the subjective (psychic) states of the observer..."

—C. G. JUNG, FOREWORD;
THE I CHING, OR BOOK OF CHANGES
(THE RICHARD WILHELM TRANSLATION)

Also by Donald Beagle

Poetry Collections

North of the Sky
Hopwood Award 1977, "major poetry" top prize
Bishop's House Press
Duke University (1987)
(limited edition chapbook)

Verses from the Multiverse
Bishop's House Press
Duke University (1988)
(limited edition chapbook)

What Must Arise
Library Partners Press / ZSR Library
Wake Forest University (2017)

Driving into the Dreamtime: New & Selected Poems
Library Partners Press / ZSR Library
Wake Forest University (2020)

Academic Books

The Information Commons Handbook
ALA / Neal-Schuman (2006)

Poet of the Lost Cause
with Bryan Giemza
University of Tennessee Press (2008)

Radcliffe Squires: Selected Poems 1950–1985
Library Partners Press / ZSR Library
Wake Forest University (2017)

The Hopwood Poets Revisited:
Eighteen Major Award Winners
Library Partners Press / ZSR Library
Wake Forest University (2018)

A Note on the Chromotints

The illustrations accompanying these 64 hexagram poems are expressions of synchronicity. The chromotints were not created as artistic interpretations of the poems, nor do the poems interpret the art.

Instead, as I worked on the poems, Ms. Merritt let me repeatedly browse the stream of new images in her draft sketchbooks. Each time, I selected one that seemed intuitively related to whatever hexagram I happened to be writing at the time. By the time my writing was complete, I had included more of Merritt's finished works (watercolors, oils, collages, and assemblages), though a fair number of the emergent sketches remain. I also included a very small number of my own photographs in the finished book. One might think of these as images floating in a perceptual space midway between the poems and their hexagrams.

Acknowledgments

Hexagrams 47, 48, and 50, sequenced under the title "An Entropic Eulogy in Three I Ching Hexagrams" appear in *CONSILIENCE* (No. 8; Spring 2022)

Hexagrams 21, 22, and 23, sequenced under the title "The Goodbye Voice," appear in *VALLEY VOICES: A LITERARY REVIEW*. (Vol.23 No.1; Spring 2023)

Hexagrams 3, 5, 6, 7, 8, 12, 16, 20, and 28, sequenced under the title "A Meditation in Nine I Ching Hexagrams" won a prize in the 2022 Ekphrasis Poetry Contest at Oakland University

Contents

Introduction

INTERVIEW WITH DONALD BEAGLE

Tell us about your new collection, *HEXAGRAMS: A POET'S JOURNEY THROUGH THE I CHING*. **I've heard through the literary grapevine that you've introduced a new stanza format never used before. That's remarkable, given the long history of versification in English.** *HEXAGRAMS* is a series of 64 six-line poems. The phrase-structures of these 64 poems cause their lines to fall into patterns of broken and unbroken segments that embody the equivalent graphic patterns of the I Ching hexagrams—the ancient Chinese system of divination. As example, **Hexagram #12,** *P'i*, means "standstill." My poem #12 shows how phrase-structure can embody the iconography of three unbroken lines above three broken lines while exploring my personal interpretation of "standstill":

> *P'i*: I reach a standstill, standing upon a ledge above the river
> still following its curving course, from distant mountains down
> eroding channels toward the sea. All things move while stand-
>
> | ing still, in oscillation with | internal particles, all quivering |
> | in an echoic intensity. As | everything shifts I'm drifting in |
> | the river flowing wider as | it loses speed to a rippling sea. |

When and how did you first envision this project?
In my sophomore year at the California Institute of the Arts, Fall 72-Spring 73. I took a course with Marshall Ho'o, Professor of Oriental History. After he discussed I Ching in historical

context, I approached him after class describing my early study of the Jung-Wilhelm translation and interpretation. He agreed to offer me a tutorial on I Ching, and I began sketching out some early versions of a few "hexagram poems." Professor Ho'o was very intrigued by those early drafts. But the project retreated to the back of my mind until two recent events rekindled my interest: I was interviewed about my CalArts experiences by Paul Cronin for his prospective book celebrating the Institute's 50th anniversary. (Paul's previous books include *A Time to Stir: Columbia '68*, about Columbia University in the late 1960's, and a collection of his conversations with filmmaker Werner Herzog). Then, through sheer coincidence of timing (or synchronicity?), I also ran across the painting "I Ching Variations" by Gian Luigi Delpin (Saatchi Art). Seeing the 64 hexagrams in Delpin's large geometric design sparked my idea to life again.

Divination has always interested me. On one level it brings to mind the prophetic tradition of the Old Testament, with its Jeremiad warnings of apocalypse or transfiguration. On another level, it offers an interesting way of reconsidering science in a socio-cultural context. The test of a scientific theory, after all, is how well it makes successful *predictions*. Science and divination share that interesting boundary: both take a considered and expectant stance toward the future.

For instance, we live in a time when predictions of climate disruption too often go unheeded or disbelieved. Among traditions of divination, the I Ching seems the most apropos to this, by way of hexagrams contrasting the actions of "the wise man" and "the foolish man." This, to me, speaks to the personae of scientists vs. politicians. For instance, I threw 3 hexagrams when I was ruminating on the trope of climate change: *K'un*: **"Oppression (Exhaustion)"**, *Ching*: **"The Well,** and *Ting*: **"The Cauldron."** I sequenced these three in a separate poem titled "Entropic Eulogy in Three I Ching Hexagrams," which recently appeared in the "Entropy" issue (#8) of *CONSILIENCE*. But my complete *Hexagrams* collection will explore other intersectionalities between science and divination. For instance, one poem notes how Gottfried Liebniz conceptualized the binary code of the future through his own musings on the I Ching, while another ponders how the genetic code includes 64 possible permutations, or *codons*, of the 3-letter nucleotide sequences.

Do your hexagrams constitute in any sense an accurate translation of I Ching?

No, absolutely not. I think "accurate translation" implies a detached objectivity, and that was most certainly not my goal. In writing these 64 poems, I am reinterpreting images and metaphors *subjectively*, filtering them through my own life experiences, which is how Jung suggested I Ching could best be approached. I've been especially influenced by the article, "Use of the I Ching in the Analytic Setting," by Dennis Merritt, Ph.D. (no relation to Meredith Joy Merritt) (*QUADRANT*; XXXI Summer 2001.)

< https://www.ecojung.com/brief-psychotherapy-a-jungian-approach >

For instance, Merritt's concept of archetypes evoked through I Ching consultations influenced my inversions of some hexagrams from positive to negative. **Hexagram #50**: *Ting*: **"The Cauldron"** is an auspicious archetype in the original texts. But in thinking about our future amid climate disruption, "Cauldron" was one of three images returned by my yarrow stalks. So my poetic rumination inverts this original archetype to explore its negative implications. Looking deeper, this inversion is not arbitrary; it grows organically from an auspicious cauldron in the sense that modern culture has created a dizzying cauldron of material possessions, based on unprecedented mass consumption and unsustainable exploitation of fossil fuels and other natural resources. So my interpretation is that an auspicious cauldron favorable to prosperity may run amok through unchecked materialism and invert to a dark cauldron of climate disruption.

On a related angle, Merritt comments: "*…working with hexagrams gives one a sense of how dream images and associations express archetypal themes. An archetype is like a crystal, each facet illustrating how the archetype would look were it presented here as a political situation, there as a military tactic, elsewhere as a weather formation, etc. Wilhelm's translation in particular helps to cultivate an archetypal sense. As mentioned earlier, the I Ching's agricultural, weather and seasonal analogies can help develop an ecopsychological perspective, a symbolic way of relating to our environment…*" This perspective may help readers understand why these 64 poems include reflections on climate, politics, metaphysics, music, pop culture, and history. I've crafted poems that weave subjectively among diverse images and metaphors.

I've also approached this project as a venue for stylistic experimentation. On one level, this is concrete poetry, where lines and line-breaks are visual renderings of the corresponding lines in the hexagrams. But there are also three narrative sequences within the set of 64 that owe their context to the confessional tradition.

So that raises an interesting question: does *The Hexagrams* as a work consist of 64 short poems, or is it a long poem in 64 parts?

I've tried to reach beyond either limiting definition. I wanted to explore a dynamic boundary condition between the short poems / long poem distinction—mirroring lyric and narrative states of expression. As a whole, and in its 64 "parts," *Hexagrams* weaves between lyric and narrative voices in an intuitive and expressive way. Some of the 64 "stanzas" first emerged as seemingly discrete creations, but others later flowed into sub-sequences whose imagery overlapped one another in a meta-narrative sense. This was especially true in three life experiences when I actually queried the oracle at times when I felt a keen interest in the future.

1: Hexagrams 21, 22, 23, 24: One day in my 30's I was giving a speech (experiencing no nervousness or stress) when my voice simply quit working. This was later diagnosed as "adult-onset dysphonia," and my voice has never returned to its original resonance over the decades since. Disturbed and distressed by this sudden problem, I threw the yarrow stalks and emerged with **Hexagram #21: "Shih Ho: Biting Through."** This seemed eerily appropriate, as these interpretive quotes from the Jung / Wilhelm edition indicate: "Shih Ho is the image of teeth biting through what is blocking communication…" Only years later I sensed a longer sequence flowing from this, through **#22: "Grace"** (or loss of), through **#23: "Splitting off"** (of self from speech), ending in **#24: "Returning"** (waiting for hope to return).

2: Hexagrams 31, 32, 33, 34, 35, 36, 37: This sequence emerged many years ago when my first wife and I learned we were expecting a new baby. I threw the yarrow stalks and cast another eerily appropriate hexagram, #31: "Wooing." It was only years later writing this collection that I realized how the following hexagrams, ending with **#37: "Family,"** seemed apropos for a narrative sequence about the final weeks culminating in the experience of our daughter's birth.

3: The third sequence evokes the diagnosis and treatment of my wife's malignant brain tumor, starting from **#39: "Obstruction,"** through **#40: Removal of obstruction, #41: Decreased intensity, #42: "Increasing progress, #43: "Breakthrough,"** and finally **#44: "Coming to meet."**

When you learn you are expecting a child, your mind turns to the future, implying an appeal to divination. When you have a diagnosis of cancer, your mind again turns to the future, evoking a different desire for divination. So the very process of writing *Hexagrams* brought to the surface certain critical life events that had caused me to interrogate my philosophical stance toward the future, and through that, the subjective significance of divination.

That is also why, through these three life sequences, I doubled (or paired) the hexagrams to approximate a sense of their past / future dualities. The first hexagram of each pair explores how I felt at that time, wondering about the future. The second hexagram of each pair casts that past event in a shifted perspective, pondering philosophical implications of those lived experiences.

And are you really the first poet to accomplish this?

UK poet Alan Baker wrote a long poem titled *The Book of Random Access,* playing off the role of randomness in I Ching divination imagery. It is an interesting work, but Baker made no attempt to craft his textual phrase-structure to embody the flux of patterning in the I Ching's sequencing of divided and undivided lines. Structurally, Baker's work is more simply composed of 64 quasi-paragraphs. It is poetry, not prose, but it features no personification of the ideographs.

And Marco Fraticelli has been issuing a series of haiku chapbooks, each of which displays an I Ching ideograph on its cover. But again, there is no attempt to *textually* embody the interplay of yin and yang across a continuum of space and time.

HEXAGRAMS

1

Ch'ien: The sun ascends as trees entangle themselves
in clouds of dusky growth, while runners of the dawn
dwindle to Lilliputians racing away from where I stand
until they fall through a small warp in the painted wall
of morning. Dragons lurk beyond each vanishing point
over heaven's horizon watching souls falling into light.

Thicket

2

K'un: I walked by childhood upon a one-lane gravel road
carved between dusky tree trunks huddled to each side.
A lost child walks in a circle it is said, dreaming direction.
Yet I am always following a lone path walking on toward
an unknown destination. Is time passing through me as I
pass within time? Or is time turning in me like a tree-ring?

Time Revisited

3

Chun: We wonder where   a road in this receptive forest
will lead. We see a luminous sky stare down at us as if it sees
where this walk will end   up taking us sooner or later or
perhaps never, if we fall   from a precipice or heartbreak
failing to foresee where   each decision sends dominoes
falling in differing directions from every tipping-point in time.

Interstices

4

Meng: "Youthful Folly" was a well in the weedyard of the
ghostly farm-house we   risked our lives in, playing as
children. Its gray wood   shaft-cover had rotted away.
We would stand round   the O of its maw, stare down
through ominous darkness below, imagining that fear of
horrific creatures rising   emerging in our nightmares.

Falling Stars

5

Hsü: Here, life is waiting   as water waits for sail-boats
to pass over its open face along trails that parallel the veils
of birds across gray skies   as I wish I could discern their
assignations. See how inscrutable arrays of boats and birds
are divulging their directions, but never their destinations,
leaving me in need of divination, or a shaman, or an omen.

Fishing Trip

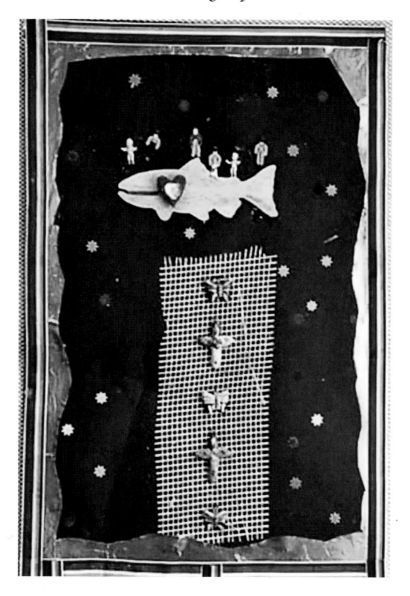

6

Sung: If the I Ching hexagrams were Rorschach charts I'd see
our pasts and futures aligned in elemental gradients of time,
where each unbroken line is from a time we took action, did
or said anything; where   open lines define things said
or done to us. In a mindspace, all things said and done to us
leave imprinted inkblots   like recursive Mandelbrots.

Nubles

7

Shih: As we stand in lines   where we wait for time to turn
our way for movie tickets,   tables at restaurants, boarding
airline flights, I think lines   trace our lives across the graph
of causality—and I wonder   which line leads covertly to the
dragon's lair. We waited once for an airplane—it never arrived
but instead dived to earth   after intersecting lines of birds.

Meditation

8

Pi: She sees how line-curves   across my palm seem to spell
lifelined letters *HE* diagonal to the tangent letter *X*. Where they
intersect some bizarre thing   may be waiting to happen, or
perhaps not—depending on   whatever may have happened
the day before, or whatever   may be waiting to happen the
following day. I flee a vexed   palmreader feeling perplexed.

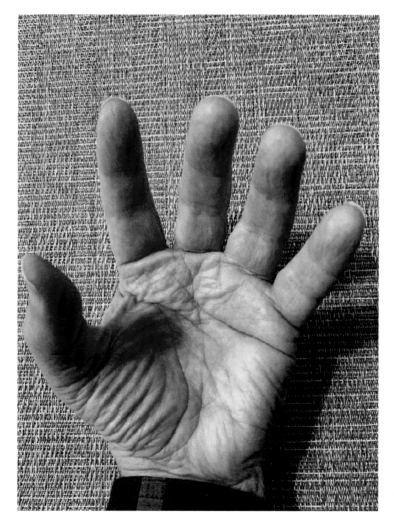

Palm

9

Hsiao Ch'u tells us the force of the small. Where I now rest in morning contemplation, the sun is sending small light-arrows piercing the parlor window.   From the sun's enormity its infinitesimal rays find each grass blade, every green tree-leaf, all the myriad flowers of every color. My window: a square of awakened light surrounded by dark walls of a deep unknown.

Sprout

10

Lü: Heaven floats over a still lake. A dream of unending life will invisibly evaporate from the cooling waterline up through heat that lifts it toward the infinite cold of space. In this way a song arises from silence as a solo   voice divests itself of weight. We hear a song hover over silence as we imagine heaven afloat above our tiring days, retiring nights, our trials of love and hate.

High Tide

11

T'ai: My wife is in a Buddhist *sangha*, and meditates each day upon the Eightfold Path. Is a life of eight directions the way a pilgrim finds the peace that surpasses understanding? Do six lines written every day for months in summer bring the mind into a peace released from understanding? Any enigmatic hexagram I reflect on makes me wonder if what I reflect reflects back on me.

Tendrils

12

P'i: I reach a standstill, standing upon a ledge above the river still following its curving course, from distant mountains down eroding channels toward the sea. All things move while standing still, in oscillation with   internal particles, all quivering in an echoic intensity. As   everything shifts I'm drifting in the river, flowing wider as   it loses speed to a rippling sea.

Light Corridor

13

Jung tells us *T'ung Jêng* means "fellowship with men." As I scan the unbroken lines across the higher trigram, I can understand how I walked the furrowed rows of freshly ploughed fields and felt fellowship with farmers I never knew. Walking those rows as a child I had seen fossils   emerge from their linear aisles of soil with curled shells unfurling millions of years to my eyes.

Party Down

14

Ta Yu: Fire in heaven flares far, and causes all things orbiting a star to be made manifest.   This is how life exists on lucky planets, yet how life persists is another vision. A heavenly fire ignites it roiling from some slimepool of time. From there, life climbs up the double-spiral laddering of nucleotides—adenine, guanine, cytosine, thymine; alternately bonding in 64 codons.

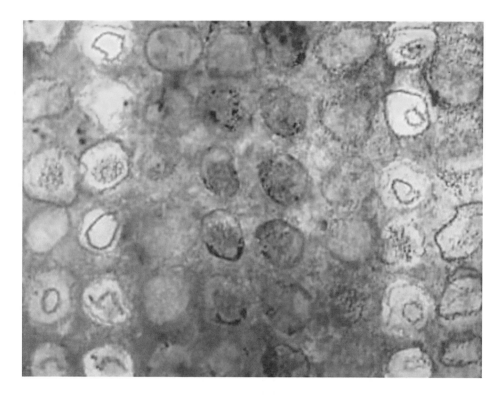

Channels

15

Ch'ien: If humility allows me   to leap 64 barriers of conceit
I must recall X. J. Kennedy's   glowing comments, Laurence
Lieberman's brilliant review   of my Hopwood Award book,
W. S. Merwin's warm responses to my Rumi sonnet sequence,
or manuscript endorsements   by Donald Hall & Marvin Bell.
But Joseph Brodsky's praise   is sealed in archives till 2071.

Open Hearts

16

Yü: At dinner in a Chinese   restaurant we sit as a family.
I find my waiting fortune-   cookie and see the split lined
down the center. There, one   end of the white paper extends
like a tongue that will tell   some truth: trivial, profound,
or neither. But after I pull   its written ribbon out like the
tongue of a tiny dragon, it   curls into a thin Mobius strip.

Quadrants

17

Sui: To set out on journeys   or to set out foods for a feast

seem similar as beginnings leading to divergent destinations.

To be a leader, one should first learn to follow—to be a ruler

one first should serve. Only   one's hunger for the sublime

upon reaching this journey's   end can bring understanding

of life's meaning in a metaphor of sharing feasts with friends.

18

Ku: Ill wind blew low near the white house, sickening all
breathing it. A pandemic   crept upon us stealthily so
that a failed president of   fools knew only squirming
worms in a bowl as those lies he fed to adoring minions
and heard only arrogant boastings of the corrupt. Greed
grinned behind the façade   of a tin flagpin on his lapel.

Stars & Twigs

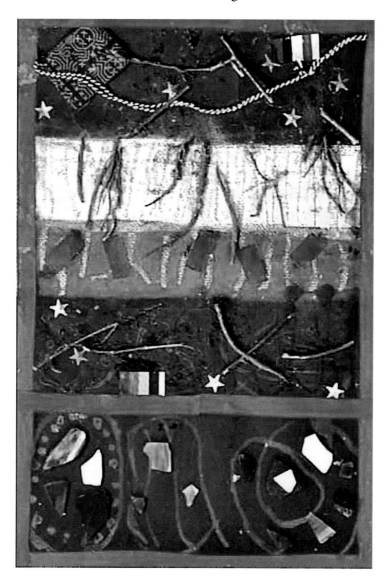

19

The present's potentialities   are emerging from the past
as the snake emerging from   a sleeve of sleep will follow
ophidian tree branches that   reach toward all interstices
from a trunk's singular mast.   Masked by earth's mephitic
coils, dark slithering roots will sprawl, weaving themselves
into the uberous soil—the spoils of all creation dying to live.

Foothills

20

Kuan, we are told, conveys a double meaning: "to be seen"
or "to be contemplative." This duality, I suspect, implies an
enigma of the observer or   the observed. Do we know
whether what we see is a   world? Or is it a world that
mirrors whatever we are?   A physicist asks if we are all
alien holograms. Or I ask   thoughts in the mind of God?

The Cat Wants to Fly

21

This hexagram, *Shih Ho*, means "Biting Through." I threw it
on saying goodbye when   my voice abruptly fractured
and fell silent, as if a line between the throat and the mind
had severed, locking up   my higher psyche in a cell of
secrecy. I rushed to the   medical clinic where I found
they had no cure for this neuromuscular curse: *dysphonia.*

What is the significance of letters along concatenated lines
of words aligned in lines   of text on pages sequencing a
flatland universe rising to a hologram only when seen between the lines? This is   the caesura where absence is
the arbiter of meaning—   the pause beyond the period
when the mind tries to read a book in the dream but fails.

Not Scared of a Scarecrow

22

Pi: A loss of voice feels like loss of grace, as if the gift
of human conversation   long taken for granted
had been split off from   its inner intentionality.
It assumes, I feel, the acceptance of a small suffering
compared to the tragic   bereavement of death.
Yet, as a poet, I fear it means demise of my persona.

Or does the goodbye voice bring transcendental life
of the mind when one   may finally hear songs
of angels aloft beyond   the wind? Is this voice
of strained whispers singing purgatory or paradise?
Perhaps I'm an auspex   poised in parallel time
entangling neurons across an etymology of change.

Cedra

23

Po: I'm given no cure, only the word "dysphonia." It

seems eerily similar to   divorce, this splitting off

of self from its speech   which, to me, was more

than a mere ornament.   If a divorce leaves a child

torn between 2 homes   my sadness goes beyond

spoken words so what   does loss of voice matter.

I write this, of course, years later, when I realize how

memory only registers   vague similes. That voice

given mine from birth   flew from the lines of my

vocal cords and out my   mouth like the final lines

of that soliloquy I once   imagined I would lament

when I found the edge   of death's final sentence.

Dormant Garden

24

Fu: Adrift in a labyrinth   of words left unspoken,
dialectics of my desires   hide unspeakably inside
the puzzled self, as I'm   like that child, tumbling
down the guttural well   toward glottal latitudes.
Voiceless, I call for help   from behind the wall of
a cylindrical jail, waiting until time turns inside-out.

When time turns inside   out, you will find a path
leading you to the edge   of a cliff, or a river, or a
cascade, or the love you   neglected in the callow
illusion of eternity. You   will find your way back
but never quite the way   you once imagined, for
the future turns its back; returns you to one final fact.

Snow

25

The *Wu Wang* hexagram, "Innocence," intrigues me,
with "Arousing Thunder" under a "Creative Heaven."
I wonder if innocent arousal might ignite a creativity
we'll fail to understand   because our religion has
insisted that innocence   was betrayed by arousal
in Eden, and again in sounds of heavenly thundering.

Our Lady of the Elements

26

Ta Ch'u: "Taming the power of the great." That window
of wakeful rays now glows   with an afternoon heat so
great it must be tamed by   dropping Venetian blinds.
These hanging horizontal slats have fenced me off from
neighbors left and right. The street whose name remains
unknown lives distantly beyond these separated splines.

White Branches

27

I: "Nourishment; Tranquility." This hexagram reminds us of
an open mouth my book   explains, and then it quotes
Mencius: "The body has   important and unimportant
parts; superior, inferior.   He who elevates an inferior
part while neglecting an   important part is an inferior
man." I ponder Mencius in the tranquility of a nice chianti.

The Path

28

Ta Quo—"A Joyous Lake   on a Gentle Wind." Every
line of text hovers over time, as in this hexagram the lake
floats over the wind. Each yarrow stalk falls in alignment
with the hidden order of randomness, as each points from
or toward the riddle of divination. But these mean nothing
other than lines of text in   your mind's oracular eye.

Fabric Composition

29

The text moves into *K'an,*   "The Abysmal," the NOW
where my meditation interrupts the interpreted world.
Water flows as the text I   read fills all places where
it fluxes. It does not stop   at a waterfall so nothing
makes it lose its essential self—coursing true to its Tao.
Lines of text flow to eyes   as time flows to its NOW.

Lightning in a Box

30

Li—"The Clinging Fire." The tiger burns in symmetry: a clinging
fire over reflecting fire. Or   is this an interference pattern
in a Confucian two-slit experiment? The beam's light illumines
four great corners of the world. But I have given no pretense
to greatness, only to best   interpret a very ordinary life;
as if an ordinary life, lived brightly, might rise in a clinging fire.

Spirit

31

Hsien: "Wooing"; the love   we'd shared as one sent
good fortune. We'd left after her water broke that night.
For weeks we'd walked by evenings, west on Greenland,
south on Woodland, wondering when birth would begin.
On returning to our house   we'd sit quietly on a bed,
inhaling, exhaling, back to   back to a new tranquility.

Was love more than a lyric   we sang to one another
in a duet? Our love arrived as an idyllic minuet, dancing
across our dream of youth—so easy to recall our melody
when words had fallen silent. Her breath became poetry
with a metrical movement   and the accompaniment
of our doubled heartbeats   in a rhyming exhalation.

The Tethered Heart

32

Hêng: "Duration—a gentle　　wind." In backward count
down we'd sound cadence　　from 9 to 1, counting out
long months of waiting. In slow motion I would help her
train her attention on feet, ankles, calves, knees, thighs,
buttocks, stomach, back, shoulders, neck, arms, elbows,
hands, fingers, practicing　　delivery of her new body.

Her woman's body lay in　　contours of my horizontal
guitar, six strings running　　long lines down its center
where, depending on the fingering, yin sings to yang and
back again. Duration here assumed the form of harmonic
progressions, centering the physical over a metaphysical
transformation, with life　　between us unified in one.

Two Hearts

33

Tun: "Retreat—in what is small perseverance furthers." In
our retreat we undertook nightly inventory of body parts.
That Lamaze lesson was relaxation. We learned to let our
bodies float on their own water like inflated boats, breath
by breath, mastering their   repertories of wind duets.
When we'd reach the end   I'd cup my ear to her belly.

When breath becomes the word exhaled into the sound of
a south wind, it carries the inflection of our ancient African
home, with a long deep drawl like slow ships trawling dark
oceans of time. What it draws up from its watery dream of
birth will quietly arise in its   cloud above the mind as
a new word for a new world   a word a new child cries.

Is Love Nearby

34

Ta Chuang—"a time when   inner worth mounts to a
great force." At times the   baby squirmed or kicked
so her flesh puckered and quivered like a water balloon.
She would exclaim "A ballet dancer!" or I'd say "A soccer
player!" But no names had yet spoken themselves to us,
so we'd say silly names like "Cleopatra" or "Theophilus."

Now, with decades gone,   when all we'd dreamed
of doing is done, our child   thrives as that one idea
worth surviving for. The single hope of her new life born
between our lives now moves on the elongated line that
already draws us toward the liminal horizon, drawing us
nearer every day, each dearer than the last but over fast.

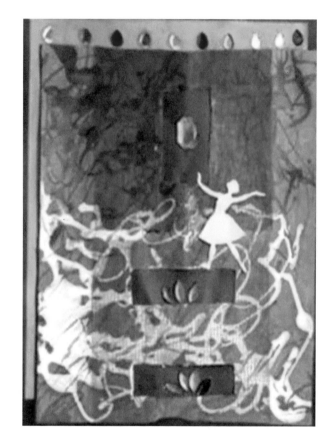

Aspiring

35

Chin—"Progress, as when the sun is seen rising over earth."
Finally that night her water   broke as our pent nerves
shifted into expectant tension. She'd say "Lets wait awhile,
I'm fine." Then I'd time the   contractions, and say "It's
faster now, should we go?"   So I drove with her singing
"This little light of mine, I'm   gonna let it shine—SHINE!"

The horizon's line at night is a trampoline upon which souls
fall from stars. Then dawn   rebounds by morning as if
all nocturnal forces fused to form the sun and rose over the
latent world. This rhythm,   like rhythmic contractions,
echoes from long epicycles   of deep time, the timeline
of tides, of pollen's season,   of cells and celestial bells.

Awake in the Dream

36

Ming I—"Darkening of light." A hospital at midnight was
apocalyptic, lit with search- lights along its roofline for
helicoptered landings. Then their ablutions initiated us,
ushering us to Maternity. I'd hoped for ease, but she entered
her labor of eighteen hours. She lay on the narrow bed
atop complex levers, grips, and gearshifts—mysterious to me.

Yet as the underworld was working its wonder a birth
must bring her to the brink of death I refused to think
about. What I cannot forget were the doors opening in
an endless corridor then closing one by one till only one shone
light for me to enter. Inside I found her strained in pain
yet fiercely laboring; a long night's drama dawning to new light.

Peasant Mask

37

Chia Jên—"Family" We held hands as she wrenched forward
and I clenched my fist to a ball behind the small of her back.
The doctor beckoned me   to look and I saw the hair
black and wet, then a thin extent of skin all bloody and pink.
Then Lucy's face dawned   with a pinched squint and
pointy ears. She did a first pirouette, eyeing us with wonder.

A line of sight, like a reversing ray of light, is where the mind
rings the penumbra of the known, fusing faces to the voices
 singing love's psalm. Its air   is the very medium of all
we hear surrounding us, the light flying as a particular wave
that rises and falls. We fall   to rise, after a cord is cut
to raise ourselves from pulsing blood, from the primal shore.

Glimpse

38

Kuei: Grotesque theatricals on tv seduce us as we end each day
lost in a labyrinth of dragons   or tigers, surrounding us for
the humor of virulent villains, or leaving us rapt among demons
of destitution. We watch the   faceless zombies obsessively
now because the walking dead remind us of a homelessness we
dread. How swiftly we could fall into a crevasse of the forgotten!

Kali Dancing

39

Chien: "Obstruction." As frost on brown December grass, or dust
on the dark glass of a window at dusk, we see the whitish treachery of
the tumor on an MRI's map of her identity. A sclerotic desiccation
of her psyche screams at us from the film's flat radius. Medieval maps
of occult oceans warned HERE BE DRAGONS. Her myelin sheathes
yield to the magnetic fields of a machine revolving like the moon.

Magnetic lines of force, curved when viewed from above, rest flat
seen from on edge, much like a windowpane of glass rests flat within its
frame, yet opens to our three- dimensional world when viewed on
either side. We see nothing until our eyes send signals over curved lines
of neural synapses that unfold images in our conceptual frames of
reference. But what of the far sides of the self, curving to infinity?

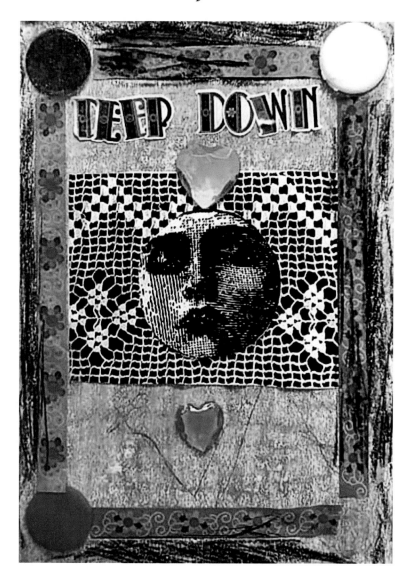

40

Hsieh: "Deliverance." The day of neurosurgery arrives. The doctor describes how the glioma has been growing near her brain's core language center with insidious jellyfish tendrils insinuating through her living cranial tissue. "You both need to prepare," he cautions her, "you may or may not be able to speak again after you wake up." Ever?? I sit in fear for hours. At last in the ICU's hallway I hear her speak!

The hours of time's elasticity seemed curved around the sphere of my fear during the surgery and left me foetal, curled to a ball of self. The waiting room expanded to a vast expanse. Seconds swelled to light-years while the clock on the wall crawled with its hands from noon to one to two to three to four to five to six to seven's mystic numeric prophecies until the neurosurgeon called for my consult.

41

Sun: "Decrease." Neurosurgery as Yin and Yang: the tumor was malign,
but early stage astrocytoma   which, the surgeon says gives hope
along with its position at the   brain's periphery. "We didn't need
to dig for it, in other words,"   he comments. But an astrocytoma
can extend miniscule filaments too tiny for an instrument to detect. We
know this means battling the dragon of radiation, the tiger of Temodar.

Here we entered a domain of astrocytes, mutating into malignant cells
with quivering tentacles, as if   we'd been at the movie and sifted
through the luminous screen   into the plot of Aliens. Or was this
the reverse where elemental   cosmic rays descended any second
by the trillions, sifted invisibly through her body, mind, and brain until
one tinged a fragile neural cell, triggering its freakish metamorphosis?

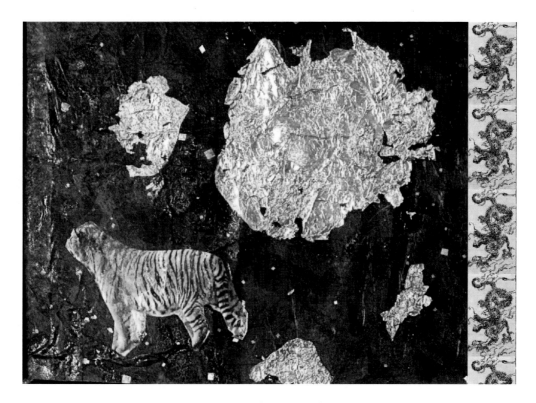

Tiger Amidst the Galaxies

42

I: "Increase." The radiation chamber clamps her on a padded sled
wearing a plastic mesh helmet on her head, yellow like a "caution
sign" with red targets marked   where the beam is aimed and
fired. The oncologists warned   us how radiation can damage
neural cells. After six weeks of   burn her words are entangled
in dysarthria. Radiation collapses brain-waves to particles of sand.

Here she becomes a brave explorer, with her plastic space helmet
on entering the Aliens' domain; a space where particles and waves
oscillating from yin to yang,   create this place where speech
shudders out of our orderly   lines of language into unknown
depths of inner anarchy. To   live here is to learn how words'
sound waves coalesce to phonons, condensing in particles of print.

43

Kuai: "Breakthrough." For six   months the doses of Temodar
leave her poisoned and distraught, imprisoned between venom
and toxin, relearning life as suffering. At last she is taken to the
MRI's planetarium, scanning her brain for magnetars or neutron
stars. The machine murmurs intonations like alien transmissions.
In a white room we wait for oncologists to welcome nothingness.

If cosmos is a universal mind   embracing all, are we rippling
out from pebbles cast in its pool of consciousness? Perhaps that is
all we ever were- undulations across a ghostly continuum of time.
Did random currents intermingle to fuse our souls? All we'll know
when our human harmonies dissipate will be a thinning theremin
spinning us toward athanasia—phasing us into phantasms of light.

Leafing

44

Kou: "Coming to meet." As I witness her long climb from dysarthria back to fluent speech, I sense her mind meeting itself anew, as if a ghost knew how to revive a comatose cocoon, reweaving threads of dormant words: frayed, knotted, or tangled. How assiduously she labors to disentangle every knot, mend every fray, braiding phonemes into an investiture of prayer. The lines she whispers grow linear vines,⠀⠀⠀⠀⠀⠀⠀entwining forests of fractal lineage.

What I find in following her is that very forest I once wandered through—the pre-dawn groves identical to twilight glades. Is this the future or the past? No longer sure I understand the difference, I only put one foot in front of another leaving footprints fading even as they fall. Holy men pretend to never wander, walking through pretensions of belief. But wandering to me is the very essence of existence—this coming to meet⠀⠀⠀⠀⠀⠀an unknown beyond all expectations.

Corn Field

45

Ts'ui: "Gathering together." I sense   I Ching cannot be intimately explored
through poetry or prose alone. Yin and Yang of language must gather together,
koan to incantation. The prose intimated here cannot flow from any textbook.
As Prof. Theodore Haddin's review   of my last book mentions: "Beagle's
long lines have taken the modern   tendency of prose to be poetry to a
high degree where prose enters a   realm of a poetic [meta] technique."

Dreamtime Cover

46

Shêng: "Pushing upward." A Book   of Changes cannot look the same
from beginning to end. As I assay   each hexagram's phenomenology
I see some broken and unbroken   lines as divination signs, designed
to define singular visions. Others live in layers like shells in beds of shale.
When a level lifts up its shadows rise sequentially over the mind's archive
as flipping pages send a series of   sketches into flickering afterlives.

Edisto Island

47

K'un: "Oppression; Exhaustion."   A lake is baked, a desiccated skein.
This dead lake-bed in the far west is the warning of dire times, the future
of oppressive heat from our atmosphere stressed with CO_2's exhaustion.
A fool will ridicule "fake news"   claiming it is not happening, even
in summers too torrid for jets to fly from Arizona airports, or as 500-year
floods horrify every five years.   Then icecaps liquify until they die.

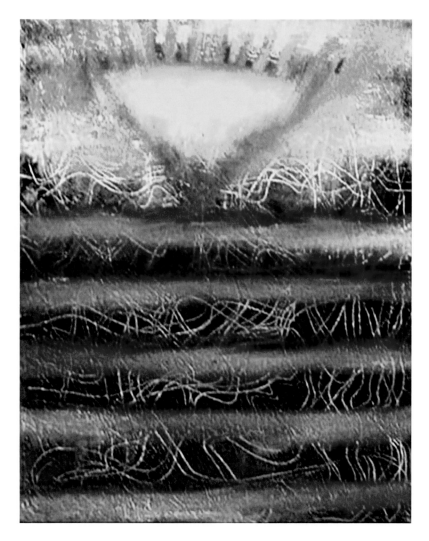

Gold Ring

48

Ching: "The Well." When water   is gone, the well is only a dark hole in dried ground. When air is fouled storms will explode to bomb-cyclones, fire-tornadoes, derechos. When   glaciers melt oceans surmount their unsuspecting shores. As plants lift water from the earth with fibrous roots families have rooted their lives in forests now burning to deserts. This arid fate awaits those cities of fools   denying science or scorning wisdom.

Vibration

49

Ko: "Revolution (Molting)" This   is the hexagram cast by Barnabas Collins in *Dark Shadows*, opening the doors of time into 1897 from 1969. The very year the vampire molted time, cosmologist Fred Hoyle predicted parallel times as pigeon-holes in a linear continuum of a multidimensional plenum. Gottfried Liebniz gazed   through I Ching to foretell binary code. Physicist Neils Bohr fashioned his coat-of-arms around Yin and Yang.

Window

50

Ting: "The Cauldron." Roiling round our world the fearsome cauldron swirls recoiling over earth as life unfurls   its rituals. The cauldron's heart beats in a slowing entropic spin, engulfing weak and hapless lives within; the lives submerged in searing, deafening din. Hieronymus' Dragon erupts wherever wildfires flare, while Blake's Tyger roars with anger through the whirlwind of a fire tornado turning the world to   dust around us, as a cauldron swirls.

Dragons in Real Time

51

Chên: "The Arousing Shock, Thunder." "In fear and trembling
one should set one's life in order, examining oneself." Three
kinds of shock are manifest; the shock of heaven's thunder, shock
of outward fate, and shock of the inward heart. A heart, we
know, is electrical; just as a lightningbolt splits air to thunder
the shock of the heart's inner torment can rend the body asunder.

Desert Lightning

52

Kên: "Keeping still, Mountain." This hexagram turns to the task of keeping a quiescent heart.　When one is calm, the mind can emerge from self-distraction　to attend an imagined forest of fallen trees that made no sound, unless we were there listening to falling sounds, witnessing　trunks across soundless ground. The sounds of tall mountains　are too enormous to be known.

Peaks of Otter

53

Chien: "Development, Gradual Progress." Within a cathedral themes
of Bach's Dorian Fugue reflect to me how the giant pyramids of Giza
were built over decades of gradual   yet monumental levels angled
toward three stars in the belt of Orion. Bach's ascents sound celestial
inspirations as his layering of slow   tonalities erects this edifice of
of vast dimensions rising over dull   gravity as time hastens slowly.

Desert Moons

54

Kuei Mei: "Thunder over waters"   as we saw the Saturn 5 climb its
pillar of fire. In their tiny capsule   atop the rocket sat the trinity of
fragile mortals, reminding us how "destiny" and "destination" conjoin
beginnings and ends. A black sky   surrounds the spinning compass
orbiting a hexagram captioned "A Marrying Maiden." A Lunar Goddess
mourns the memory of 1969, when human boots stepped on the moon.

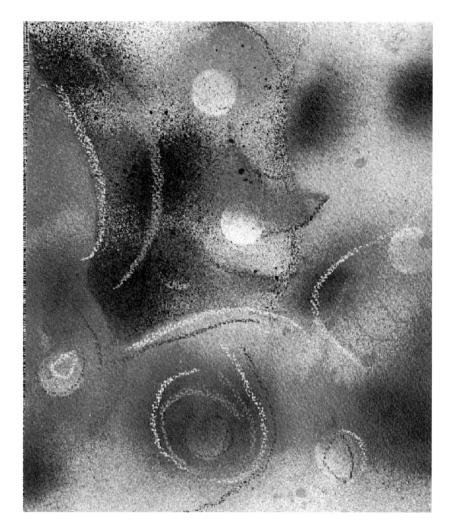

Eider Down

55

Fêng: "Abundance (Fullness)," In   good harvests on our family's farm,
I knew, during the late 1950's, I   was witnessing the slow passing of
an era, and I was grateful to wake and sleep so near to the dear earth. We
all sensed, somehow, that we were privileged pilgrims, baling the hay from
reaping at each season's harvest.   Over cool autumns we visited cider
mills on horseback. Our neighbors drew water turning a tinblade windmill.

Unfurling

56

Lü: "The Wanderer." So it is said, "A wanderer has no fixed abode, his home is the road." Every   August we would leave home to vacation in Michigan's Upper Peninsula. There, I would wander the Lake Superior shorelines from Whitefish Point west to Grand Sable Dunes. The water was frigid   to swim in, but clear as the glass of a telescope lens. Through   it I saw swirled and spiral agates.

Riot

57

Sun: "The Gentle (Penetrating Wind)." Wind from Lake Superior is rarely gentle, but even then, is penetrating with the north's sharp pointed breath, sheathed in   its gentility. So too, a laser fires from an observatory dome like a lined medieval eidolon drawn on the spine of an illuminated tome, adjusting the mirror's enormous eye to peer through angelic   air to spiraling halos of galaxies.

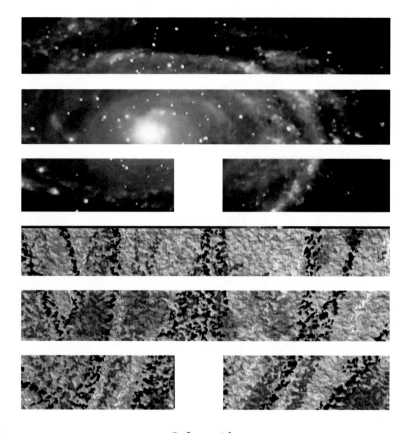

Galaxy Above

58

Tui: "The Joyous, Lake." On two cool   but beautiful days after the New Year
when she had recovered from chemotherapy enough to walk with no support
we drove north from our home to Lake Norman. The water was a blue-glazed
brown, the sky reflected from layers   of sand and tannic acid. Her smiling
gaze reflected relief from a long torment. Arm in arm we made our way along
a path between the longleaf pines whose needles pretended to be sunbursts.

Lotus

59

Huan: "Dispersion (Dissolution)." That was her last unaided walk with me as she
caught a respiratory infection. Then a scan found early blood-clots on her lungs.
She was given blood-thinning drugs.   Every night she'd watch the vampire,
Barnabas Collins, raging against the   blood—curse of Angelique, the witch
from Martinique. Surely this would pass, she'd say. Surely a cure or a recovery at
last will come to stave off this slow   dissolution. Sleep was our dispersion.

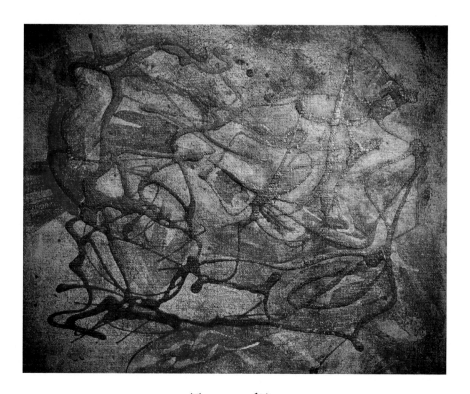

Tongues of Fire

60

Chieh: "Limitation." She walks now with the aid of wheels. She writes now with dictation. I help her as I can though my face, too, wears lines of six decades. My eyes grow "slightly cloudy," portentous as in a weather forecast. But this forecast is portending more than weather. My way through the forest is dimmer now than ever before. My hair is thinning to wisps, my knees have grown arthritic. My ears no longer hear the charming arias of youth, but whine internally as introverted insects.

Suffused

61

Chung Fu: "Inner Truth." I'm surrounded by the churlish lies of childish fools who worship their tin-god like red paladins on witchhunts. They burn down our democratic trees to erect shrines   to the Fourth Reich. Their church enshrines an altar to money-lenders.   Shall this, too, pass away? Or will the grotesque old party crown their failed charlatan as a president for life? Thus I must abhor the company of dishonorable fools to find my inner truth.

The Path

62

Hsiao Kuo: "Preponderance of the Small." As I gaze back upon the six-lined stanzas I find them widening from beginning to end much as the small rivulet slips down mountain-rocks where it begins, but soon joins other rivulets of meaning, forming creeks, then streams, then a river that broadens its banks at every corner, turning itself into a spreading estuary that never ends until becoming ocean. Yet far within its small rivulet lives.

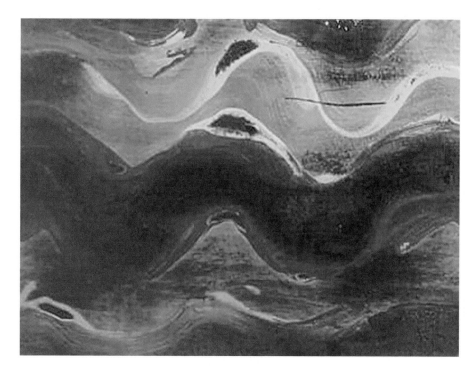

Full River

63

Chi Chi: "After Completion." The river   was here too wide for me to cross
so I turned to walk through the dusky woods to follow its bank farther along.
I veered into a clearing, but the river   was here too wide for me to cross
so I turned to walk through the dusky woods to follow its bank farther along.
I waded in a wetland, but the water   was here too wide for me to cross
so I turned to walk through the dusky woods and at last found my way across.

Through Kiawah Island

64

Wei Chi: "Before Completion." I followed the road through dusky glades until I found the river flooding.   Because I'd not abandoned hope on entering that wood, I waded till water lapsed to walk in dusky glades. I found it flooding far beyond.   Because I'd not abandoned hope on crossing that wood, I waded till water lapsed to walk in dusky glades. I find flooding farther beyond.   Never abandoning hope, I wade.

Marsh on Kiawah

Conifers on Kiawah